the Label

First published in the UK in 2017 by
Ivy Press
Ovest House
58 West Street
Brighton BN1 2RA
United Kingdom
www.quartoknows.com

British Library Cataloguing-in-Publication Data
A catalogue record for this book is available
from the British Library

ISBN: 978-1-78240-460-6

This book was designed and produced by
Ivy Press
Publisher *Susan Kelly*
Creative Director *Michael Whitehead*
Editorial Director *Tom Kitch*
Senior Project Editor *Joanna Bentley*
Copy-editor *Viv Croot*

Printed in China

10 9 8 7 6 5 4 3 2 1

the Label

A STORY FOR FAMILIES

Caroline White
with illustrations by Sandra Isaksson

IVY PRESS

I WRAPPED YOU IN your new soft, brushed blanket, and laid you down gently in your crib. You looked so tiny. I watched as you calmly drifted off into a peaceful sleep. You couldn't feel the piercing pain that filled the room, or see the tears rolling down my face. At least, I hoped you couldn't. I felt winded in the heart, unable to move, waiting to breathe, for normal life to come back. Here you were, my brand new, longed-for baby – and I didn't want you. Well, not like this anyway. Of course I felt love for you, I was poleaxed by the ridiculous amount of love I felt for this life I had carried and nurtured and daydreamed about for so long, but...

HOW WAS IT POSSIBLE to love something so deeply, with so much longing, but at the same time not want it?

Who were you? I didn't know you. You weren't what we were expecting. I couldn't just send you back, swap you for a different model. Nothing made sense. This was supposed to be the happiest time of my life, but it was the worst.

A doctor had drawn a heavy black line right through the centre of my universe, and we were on the wrong side of it. And you: you weren't the little seed packed with unknowable potential; you'd already been graded and sorted. Labelled.

We took you home. You and a few leaflets. Flying blind with broken wings and a broken heart. Yet I longed to protect you. I wanted to scoop you up, hold you tight and run away. Somewhere safe. Somewhere isolated. Somewhere hidden. Somewhere where we wouldn't feel 'different'.

And then came the books. I had a shelfload. Books I had bought, and books I had been given. Books that would tell me who my baby was, what our future held, what to expect and how to deal with it. Books that would help make it better, give me the answers – a map for the unwanted path we now had to walk. Books that would give me back some control. Manuals for you.

NERVOUSLY, I BEGAN to take them down from the shelf. If I read hard enough, maybe I could control things. I opened the first book. I pored over the words, stared at the pictures and soaked up the details, making notes obsessively. I felt guilt. I felt fear. I felt grief. I felt sick. The letters danced about on the pages, making my head hurt as I tried to picture what lay in store for us. With every new piece of information, the enormity of what our lives would be like sunk deeper into my heart, the burden growing heavier and heavier.

I looked at you, ticking off every physical characteristic listed on your label's small print — and yet all I could see was your dear little face. You didn't know you had a label. How was I going to tell you? Panic and grief ambushed me. Your dad found us, you and me, your plump little cheeks awash with my tears. He said gently, 'You're his mum, you're his biggest backer. You can't expect the world to accept him, if you can't. Imagine the day he walks up to you and taps you on the knee and says "Hello Mum".' But I couldn't hear him; I was at the bottom of the well.

There was a knock at the door. I shuffled reluctantly to open it. A blast of icy winter air sharpened all my senses. Everything felt exaggerated. The world was grey

and cold and different. Somehow slower, but at the same time too fast. People were going about their daily lives, doing the school run, popping to the shops, talking about the government... I couldn't believe it. How could things be so normal?

A man stood on the doorstep. He was smiling reassuringly, and in his hands was a parcel, neatly wrapped in brown paper. The size and shape told me immediately that it was another book. Another book. I sighed. Suddenly aware of my self-absorption, I made eye contact, smiled back at him and reached out to take the package.

FOR A MOMENT we were connected, the man and I, each holding one end of the package. As our eyes met, a link was forged between us. For a millisecond it seemed he wasn't going to let go. Suddenly I wanted to tell him everything, spill out my pain. Then he released his hand, and the parcel was mine. A cold flurry of wind stirred up the dead leaves on the ground. Litter looped and swirled down the street. Something on the package flapped and flickered, determined to tear itself away. It was a note or a label, but before I could see what it was, it broke free. I tried to grab it, but it danced away joyfully upwards.

I stretched out my arm, stood on tiptoes, desperate to catch it, to find out what was on it, but it was out of my reach. It flew up and up into the dreary sky, darting and spiralling round and up, getting smaller and smaller and rising higher and higher into the greyness. Like a baby bird leaving its nest for the first time, it gathered speed and confidence as it soared. It was a tiny dot. Eventually it disappeared altogether.

I shut the door. We were back in our small world. I placed you in your crib, and looked at the package. I wanted to savour a moment of peace before opening it. The label was lost, there was no other clue as to who

the book was from. I unpicked the tightly tied string,

and the paper fell to the floor to reveal the gift inside.

There was no accompanying card nor comforting note,

nor fancy wrapping.

Just the book.

I T WAS A PLAIN HARDBACK BOOK. It was clean and smooth. There was no title. The enigmatic blankness of it offered some respite and calm. I stroked the cover, it was cool to the touch. I lifted it to my face and pressed it against my hot cheek, enjoying a few brief seconds of tranquillity. This was it. I had a very strong feeling, a mother's instinct, that this was the book that would give me all the answers I wanted. I cradled it lovingly as if it were the baby I had been expecting. I took a deep breath, and slowly, tentatively, opened the pristine front cover.

Blank page… blank page… blank page…

Page after page. Clear, empty space. I kept on turning and turning – another clean, crisp, white page. And another. At first, the empty space offered relief to my hot, sore eyes. I sat enjoying the calm until I had the energy to turn another page, and another, and another. *Still blank.*

I started searching frantically for the words, in case I had missed them. Each and every page was empty. There was nothing for us – you and me – here. I was confused and disheartened.

Angry. Exhausted. Terrified. Cheated. Hurt. Broken.

Again.

IT WAS THE SMALL SOUND of you crying that jolted me back to reality. I scooped up all the books, including the infuriating blank one, and stacked them on the shelf. I'd had it with books. I picked you up and realized just how much I had missed you while you were sleeping. I kissed your sweet face, and was suddenly overwhelmed. I held you tight, so close to me I could feel your heart beating, your brave vulnerability sending an electric bolt through my own broken heart. Guilt and love flooded me. I hoped desperately that you would never know what I had been thinking. I silently vowed I would always, always protect you.

THE BOOKS WERE MOVED to a higher shelf. They collected dust. I didn't care what they said and eventually I forgot about them. You were my new study. Every day, bit by bit, you grew a little more, and so did I. Every day, I noticed something new and enchanting about you. I cheered as we passed every milestone, burst with joyful pride at every achievement and celebrated every mountain we climbed. We started to find our own way. Together.

You smiled, you cried, you walked, you talked. One day, it did happen, just as your dad said it would: you tapped me on my knee and said 'Hello Mum'. Nothing could stop you. You sang songs and made jokes, you played football and rode a scooter. You went to school and loved to race against the wind on your bike. You liked sausages and chips and ice cream, and splashing in the sea. You hated having your hair washed and going to the dentist. You built sandcastles and went on bear hunts. You dreamt of becoming an astronaut. You marvelled at rainbows and jumped in puddles. You devoured every new experience with a wonderful greedy enthusiasm and lust for life, stopping to smell the flowers and stroke every dog that crossed your path. You were a son, a grandson, a nephew and a cousin. You were a friend and a class-mate. You were a student and a teacher. And soon, you were promoted to big brother.

YOUR LITTLE FACE WAS full of magic and mischief and you filled my life with a richness that I could never have imagined possible. You grew from a baby to a boy and from a boy to a man. You taught me so much and changed the way I looked at everything. You were the son I had always dreamed of and instead of dreading the future I was now excited by it. The only pain in my heart was caused by my pride in you, bursting out from every corner. You were driven and hard-working. You thrived on success. You became independent, you got a job, you had a social life and a partner… and sooner than I expected, or wanted, suddenly, it was time for you to cut the strings.

mum

WE PLANNED AND PACKED. You took your faithful toy dog, with you since the day you were born, your football season ticket, the photo of you and your siblings laughing heartily, and your favourite pyjamas. And I kept in my heart the tender, bittersweet moment all mothers feel when their first-born steps out into the world. As we finished packing, I was swept away by the same confusing mixture of emotions that I had felt when you were just a baby. I didn't want you to go, I would miss you so much. You wouldn't be far away but I wanted to hold on to you forever and never let you go.

But I knew I had to.

WHEN YOU HAD GONE, to fill the void, I started sorting through the house. After a while I came across the books that had seemed so important to me all those years ago. They were still on the top shelf. One by one I took them down, out of date and dusty. I flicked through each one and they took me back to those early, dreary days when you were new and I was distraught and full of guilt and self-loathing, trapped in the well.

Looking at them now, I found it impossible to believe that I had ever been so fearful of our lives together, that I had not understood who you were, or who you would become. Had I really assumed you would be like a chapter in a textbook, or a page in a leaflet? Had I really been so sad about having you?

Reality had been so far removed from those fearful visions. Reality had been a life enriched with happiness and wonder, depth and meaning, richness, value and belonging. A life and journey I would not swap for the world.

And what about the book with no label? I was no longer angry at its betrayal, but still puzzled by its meaning. It was right at the back of the shelf. I had to stand on tiptoes on a chair to reach it. As I slid the book out, there was a flutter of loose paper and a scattering of shiny dust that glistened and danced in the sunlight. The book was bulkier and heavier than I remembered and I almost dropped it. I barely recognized it. Despite spending years unopened and untouched, it was no longer smooth and pristine, but dog-eared... and stuffed fit to bursting. Memories, photos, bits and bobs, snippets and scribbles...

PAGES AND PAGES, no longer blank, but a chronicle of joys and wonders, heartaches, frustrations and achievements. Our lives together. Every precious moment captured, a book filled with smells and sounds and colours. Laughter and tears. A book with personality and life. Stained and smudged. Loved. The first day you walked, your first word, the day you started school, the day you learned to ride a bike, grazed knees and tears, holidays and Christmases. The day you got lost at the safari park and I was physically sick with fear. Letters to the Tooth Fairy. Your first love, the first job. Football-pitch birthday cakes and plane journeys to Australia. Racing your brother and sister to the house.

A broken arm, visits to Grandma's. Good times and tough times. Season tickets and train tickets. Top of the league and bottom of the league. Grit and glitter. Grains of sand and seashells. Certificates and celebrations.

And in one tiny moment I realized that this was the most important book, the book I had been looking for when you first came. A book filled with memories and precious moments. A unique lifetime, shaped by our own personal journey and not the path we had been told we would follow. A book with dimension, depth and meaning that had evolved constantly over time and was full of love and learning.

A book without a label.

ABOUT THE AUTHOR

Caroline White lives with her husband and three children in Bath, England. Her eldest son, Seb, was unexpectedly diagnosed with Down's syndrome 24 hours after his birth. Initially devastated by the news, Caroline soon began to realise her view of Down's syndrome was very outdated and has made it her mission to try to change attitudes that still surround the condition. She writes a blog and works for many charities to help try and achieve this. She has campaigned for more inclusive advertising, and in 2012 Seb made history as the first child in the UK with Down's syndrome to feature in a major high street retailer's TV ad when he starred in Marks & Spencer's Christmas TV campaign. Seb has also modelled for Kinder chocolate, Jojo Maman Bébé, Muddy Puddles, Sainsbury's and Fujifilm.

Caroline has appeared on TV and radio news programmes, been featured in many broadsheets and spoken at a TedX event hosted by Kings College London. She is a family ambassador for Mencap and an ambassador for the Special Olympics GB.

AUTHOR'S ACKNOWLEDGEMENTS

Thank you to my family and friends, especially my mum and my husband, Simon, for all your words of wisdom and for just being there. Thank you to all the professionals, carers, teachers, parents and advocates who champion inclusion and campaign for equality. A huge thank you to Sandra for her generous support and for making this the beautiful book I hoped it would be.

And most of all, thank you Sebastian, Dominic and Polly.

Mencap is the UK's leading learning disability charity. Everything we do is about valuing and supporting people with a learning disability, and their families and carers. Our vision is a world where people with a learning disability are valued equally, listened to and included. For more information about Mencap and learning disability, visit www.mencap.org.uk